MUSHROOMS
AND
TOADSTOOLS
By
JACQUELINE SEYMOUR

Designed by
DAVID GIBBON

Produced by
TED SMART

COLOUR LIBRARY INTERNATIONAL

INTRODUCTION

Many people think of fungi as members of the plant kingdom but there is a fundamental difference between them and green plants. Green plants are able to make organic compounds necessary for photosynthesis, which can only occur in the presence of the green pigment, chlorophyll. Fungi do not possess this pigment. Some obtain their food by breaking down dead plant or animal material, in which case they are known as saprophytes or saprobes; others grow parasitically on living plants and animals. A number of species form an association with the roots of trees, which is a reason why certain kinds are regularly found growing near particular species of tree. The fungus either grows tightly round the tree roots or it can penetrate the roots and grow inside them. Such fungus roots are called mycorrhiza. The fungus receives nutrients from the tree and in its turn enables the tree roots to absorb otherwise unavailable minerals from the soil. This confers an advantage to both fungus and tree; such an association for the mutual benefit of the partners is known as symbiosis.

Mushrooms and toadstools are the fruiting bodies of fungi and represent only a short stage in their life cycle. These produce thousands of spores which eventually germinate giving rise to fine branched thread-like structures called hyphae. As these filaments continue to grow they form a mass known as mycelium, which can remain unnoticed. (It is this mycelium which forms the mycorrhiza in symbiotic fungi). When conditions are right for spore formation the familiar mushrooms and toadstools appear. They too are made of hyphae, in this case densely interwoven. They grow, the spores mature and are released giving rise to new mycelia and the cycle has begun again.

There are some 200,000 species of fungi, many of which have a wide geographical distribution. Assuming that the correct habitat exists a given species of fungus can be found growing almost anywhere in the world provided that temperature and moisture levels are adequate for germination and growth. The fungi make up a large and varied group which includes such members as the mould *Penicillium notatum* (from which the first antibiotic penicillin was produced), rusts, smuts and mildews and yeasts such as those used to make bread rise and to make alcoholic drinks such as beer and wine. Such fungi are generally small and inconspicuous, if not actually microscopic, even when fruiting bodies are present, and the following pages are therefore concerned with their showier relatives.

The distinction between mushrooms and toadstools is an artificial one which has no biological significance. It has been said that edible fungi were called mushrooms and poisonous ones toadstools. It will be obvious from the first sections of this book that this distinction does not apply. Indeed later pages illustrate toadstools which are inedible merely because they are unpalatable and not because they are poisonous.

There are illustrated here a number of fungi which are described as edible. It cannot be emphasized too strongly that extreme care should be taken to ensure that a specimen is correctly identified before it is consumed. Fungi can be particularly difficult to identify because one species can vary enormously in shape, size and colour, especially when immature. It is therefore wise to gather only fully grown (but not old) specimens. When picking fungi of which the identity is doubtful the whole growth should be picked even if the stipe (stalk) is to be discarded later. This very often allows a firm identification to be made at home with the help of a comprehensive reference book. It is also extremely unwise to assume that a group of fungi growing fairly close together all belong to the same species, and each specimen should be individually examined to confirm its identity. Only perfect specimens should be gathered and no picking should be done while wet as decay will set in very quickly.

As with other foods palatability is very much a question of personal preference; some people may find certain species distasteful while others enjoy them. Similarly some kinds of fungus generally considered edible may disagree with some people in the same way as, for example, shellfish do. It is only sensible to have a small helping of a fungus that is new. While some fungi make excellent dishes in their own right some are more suitable for flavouring such things as soups and stews and others are particularly useful when dried.

People living in continental Europe, particularly in France, commonly eat a number of different fungi. For those who wish to do the same it is vital to remember that a number of generally held beliefs are dangerously wrong. A toadstool which "peels" is not necessarily edible. The prized Field or Meadow Mushroom does indeed peel, but so too does the deadly poisonous Death Cap. It is a fallacy that blanching (boiling in water) renders all harmful species safe, although this certainly does apply to some, as drying does to others. A toadstool which changes colour when the flesh is broken is not necessarily dangerous. Species of *Boletus* do this, turning a vivid blue, and even Field Mushrooms show colour changes. Colour is of no significance in determining whether a fungus is poisonous or not, but it is, of course, invaluable as an aid to identification.

There are few widely recognised English names for fungal species. Even the well-known *Amanita muscaria* is called the Fly Agaric in Britain and the Fly Amanita in North America. The student of fungi has therefore to become familiar with the Latin, or scientific, names. Unfortunately even this is not without problems because scientific names are being changed as understanding of inter-relationships increases. In this text English and scientific names are given, although the former are often of curiosity value only.

Mycology, the study of fungi, is complicated but fascinating. It is hoped that this book will stimulate a further inquiry into the biology and culinary potential of fungi.

Left: Inocybe patouillardii

Deadly Poisonous Fungi

In view of the evil reputation that toadstools have it is perhaps surprising that very few are killers. Three of these are illustrated on these two pages. Illustrated on page 2 is *Inocybe patouillardii*, sometimes known as the Red-staining Inocybe. This is a very poisonous species which can be confused with the St. George's Mushroom (page 13) when it is young and white. The cap turns brick-red immediately it is bruised, and the picture shows the mature yellowish-brown toadstool. It has an unpleasant strong and fruity smell and mild taste. It is found in grass along wide paths in and at the edges of deciduous woodland, particularly beech woodland. The symptoms of poisoning include vertigo, blindness and cold sweats. Occasional deaths have been recorded.

The Death Cap *Amanita phalloides, left and below left*, is the most dangerous of the fungi shown here. It is probably responsible for 90% of the deaths in Britain from fungus poisoning. The top picture shows the young toadstool bursting through its egg-shaped sheath, the volva, in which it develops below the ground. (Presence of a volva is characteristic of all species of *Amanita*).

The flesh is white under the skin of the cap, which can vary in colour. Here it is clearly seen to be "poison" green, but it can range through shades of green and brown to white. In the adult toadstool *below* there is a ring round the stipe (stem) and the remains of the volva are visible as a bag-shaped structure. The cap peels. This fungus is found in frondose woods in autumn, particularly in oak woods but also in beech. The great danger from it lies in the fact that its effects are not noticeable for some time after eating, so standard treatments for poisoning are ineffective. Only the tiniest amount is needed to cause illness; even the spores are poisonous. Surprisingly rabbits are not affected by it; their digestive juices destroy the poison. Slugs seem to thrive on it.

The Destroying Angel *Amanita virosa, top right,* another woodland species, is found mostly under beech in summer and early autumn. It is usually wholly white and the gills remain white even when mature. It too has a bag-like volva and the cap peels. It is another deadly poisonous fungus and here again the poison is absorbed into the body before the effects are noticed. This is a rare species which explains why it is responsible for fewer fatalities than the Death Cap.

None of these toadstools, especially the last two, should be allowed the slightest contact with mushrooms being gathered to be eaten.

Below right, Ergot *Claviceps purpurea.* While it is hardly likely that anyone would actually pick this fungus and take it home to cook for supper it is of extreme agricultural and economic importance. It is parasitic on grasses, particularly rye. While very different from the toadstools previously discussed (it is a member of a different Class) this is nevertheless still the fruiting body. It is extremely poisonous causing the disease of ergotism if eaten, as it can be if infected cereals are consumed. Use of modern fungicides and careful screening of grain has virtually eliminated ergotism but the fungus is still commonly to be found on wild grasses. It is a source of valuable and important drugs.

More Poisonous Fungi

The Fly Agaric, Fly Amanita or Scarlet Fly-cap, *Amanita muscaria, left,* is the one instantly recognisable toadstool even to the complete novice. The characteristic white spots are remnants of the volva which is not as tough as that of the Death Cap or Destroying Angel and so tears easily into little pieces. It has the reputation of being extremely poisonous but this is not entirely justified as although toxic it is rarely fatal. Excitement and hallucinations are reported in some cases of poisoning but gastric symptoms are far more likely. These occur within one to three hours of ingestion. It is thought that the poison is only to be found in the skin of the cap and that peeling should therefore make it safe. The fungus has been used since mediaeval times to control flies. It was broken up and put in shallow containers of milk, which stupefied flies which drank it. *Amanita muscaria* is found in woodland, usually under birches but also under pines, in late summer and autumn.

Entoloma sinuatum, the Leaden or Livid Entoloma, *top right,* resembles the Field or Meadow Mushroom (pages 10-11) at some stages of its development. The gills are yellowish-cream at first and become salmon pink. There is no ring on the stem. The similar mushroom types grow well away from trees but *Entoloma sinuatum* is found in grassy places especially in broad-leaved woods. It causes violent sickness and diarrhoea occasionally leading to death.

Gyromitra esculenta is known as the Brain Gyromitra, False Morel or Turban Fungus, *centre.* Despite the specific name *esculenta* which means "edible" this fungus is very poisonous when raw. The poison is probably destroyed by drying and cooking. It seems possible that some strains of this species are more poisonous than others. It is much sought after in Scandinavia and Eastern Europe but it is not generally eaten in North America where it also occurs. It grows in coniferous woods in spring. When young it is a fawn colour which matures to a dark chestnut brown.

Amanita pantherina, bottom right, is called the Panther Cap, Panther Amanita or Agaric, or False Blusher. As this last name implies it can be confused with the edible Blusher (page 9). It gives rise to similar symptoms, if eaten, to those caused by *Amanita muscaria* but these appear in a more serious form. While found in autumn mainly in beech woods this is an unreliable means of identification as it can grow in a wide range of habitats.

8

All the toadstools illustrated here are poisonous (but do not generally kill) when raw, but are supposedly good and safe to eat when cooked. The risk of possible trouble does not seem to be worth taking when there are so many delicious and perfectly safe fungi to be found.

The Devil's Boletus *Boletus satanus, left,* does not deserve its name and reputation although it is probably very indigestible. It certainly exhibits a range of ominous colours. The flesh in the stem and cap reddens when exposed to the air and then slowly turns a bluish-green. All parts will turn blue when rubbed. This is a rather rare woodland species found in summer and autumn.

Russula emetica, the Sickener or Emetic Russula, is shown *top right.* The names indicate what happens if this toadstool is eaten raw. It has a pleasant smell and an acrid, peppery flavour. It is found under conifers in autumn.

The Blusher *Amanita rubescens, centre right,* is so called because the flesh becomes pink when broken (in a compact specimen the colour may take some time to develop). It is possible to confuse it with the more dangerous Panther Cap (page 7). While many species of fungus are likely to be infested with fly maggots the Blusher seems particularly prone to attack. Like all species of *Amanita* this is found in woodland, being one of the first to appear in autumn.

Bottom right, the Woolly Milk Cap or Woolly Lactarius *Lactarius torminosus.* Milk Caps are characterised by the exudation of milky fluid which occurs when the cap is damaged or broken (see page 26). One or two members of the genus *Lactarius* are highly prized as edible species, but this one acts as an irritant if eaten raw (*torminosus* means griping). As the name also suggests this milk cap is noticeably woolly. It is found in summer and autumn in woods and heathland, often near birches.

Edible Fungi

All the fungi illustrated on the next two dozen pages are edible. This emphasizes the fact that relatively few poisonous fungi exist and demonstrates the large number of perfectly safe substitutes. It should still be remembered that some kinds may disagree with some people, and caution should be exercised at first.

The Field or Meadow Mushroom *Agaricus campestris, left and top right,* must surely be the most widely collected and eaten mushroom of all. The picture on the right shows two important differences between it and species of *Amanita.* The gills are pink; they turn brown as the spores mature. There is only a narrow ring which soon falls off. A third difference is that there is no volva. The Field Mushroom grows in meadows and pastures and is never found near trees. It is found in autumn.

The Horse Mushroom *Agaricus arvensis, bottom,* is much larger and the gills are greyish not pink. It too has an excellent flavour but is much less common than the Field Mushroom. It is normally found in fields where horses have grazed but specimens are occasionally found in woods.

13

The fungi on these pages are all found in grassy places. *Coprinus comatus*, the Shaggy Ink Cap, Shaggy Mane, Lawyer's Wig or Judge's Wig, *left and below*, is a large fungus; a total height of 30 cm is not unusual and the cap itself can measure up to 12 cm in height. It is often found in clusters as in the bottom picture and commonly colonises rubbish tips. It can also be found on roadsides and cinder paths. It is very good to eat if picked while the gills are closed and the cap is white. Complete liquidisation of the gills takes place in the mature fungus, forming an inky fluid. (This process is called auto-digestion–the fungus digests itself.) The caps should be used immediately after gathering or they will begin to melt away. *Coprinus comatus* is found earlier in the year than most other species and can be gathered from late spring to late autumn.

The fungi on this page can all be found growing in fairy rings.

Fairy rings have been a subject for speculation down the ages and have been attributed to the action of fairies, witches and the like. They are visible for most of the year as rings of lush grass greener than the rest, sometimes with a bare patch either in the middle or running round as an inner circle. There is no doubt that fungi are responsible for these rings and the mechanism is fairly well understood. As the mycelium becomes established it grows out in a circle from its origin, continuing to grow out as the old mycelium in the centre dies. Only the outer edge grows, and the green ring is thought to be caused by the grass having the benefit of waste products from the fungal activity. The toadstools are formed just inside the darker ring in an area where growth of grass is usually reduced. After the mycelium dies off in the centre of the ring the vegetation returns to normal. There is a picture of toadstools growing in a fairy ring in woodland on page 15.

St. George's Mushroom *Tricholoma gambosum, top right,* is another mushroom which appears in spring. It can be found in Britain from as early as St. George's Day (April 23rd), hence its name, until June.

Blewits *Lepista saeva, centre,* is also known as Blue Leg. This is an edible late autumn species of open grassy places in and around woods. The colour is very variable and specimens can be found ranging from violet to buff.

The Fairy-ring Champignon *Marasmius oreades, bottom right,* is sometimes called the Fairy-ring Marasmius. Its old name was Scotch Bonnets because of the shape of the cap. It is small and tough but has a good flavour. Unusually resistant to drought it shrivels in dry weather but revives after rain. It is one of the best known of the many species which form fairy rings.

13

Edible Species of Woodland

Wood Blewits *Lepista nuda,* also known as the Blue Cap *left,* appears in autumn in gardens as well as in woods. The density of the colour varies with shade and moisture, and can be quite a dark violet, especially when the toadstool is young. It should be cooked before eating but it is relished and sought after, having a pleasantly aromatic taste.

Clitocybe geotropa, right, is a striking autumn toadstool often found growing in fairy rings as it is shown *below.* It is found in grassy clearings or at the edges of woods. It can reach a height and breadth of 30 cm. The stem develops before the cap, which is best eaten when young.

Honey Fungus, Honey Tuft, Honey Armillaria or Shoe-string Agaric *Armillaria mellea, far left,* is a serious and destructive parasite of many kinds of trees. Its mycelium is also responsible for the eerie luminosity sometimes seen in woodland at night.

Russula vesca, above left, is found in deciduous woods, especially oak. It is particularly prone to attack by maggots.

The Chantarelle *Cantharellus cibarius* is a well known edible fungus *below left,* which to some people smells of apricots. It is easy to recognise and it always grows in groups. It should only be cooked for a short time.

Fistulina hepatica, above, is known as the Ox-tongue or Poor Man's Beef Steak but here looks very like the liver to which it owes its specific name.

Clavaria pistillaris, the Club Clavaria or Giant Club *right,* is a fairy club found in leafy woods in autumn. It darkens when touched.

17

More edible woodland species are shown here.

Hydnum rufescens, top left, is a tooth fungus known as a Wood Hedgehog in Britain and called the Bread Roll Fungus in Germany. It is found in all kinds of woods in autumn, often in fairy rings. The spore-bearing tissue is not carried on the gills as in the Agarics but covers awl-shaped teeth under the cap. These are reminiscent of hedgehog spines, hence the popular name. This is very similar to the more common Wood Hedgehog *Hydnum repandum* (not illustrated). The cap of the latter is paler and the taste rather bitter. The bitterness can be removed by cutting up and boiling in water for about five minutes and then draining. The pieces should then be thoroughly cooked with plenty of fluid.

Bottom left, the Jew's Ear or Ear Fungus *Auricularia auricula-judae.* This gelatinous fungus is a great delicacy in China and a similar variety is grown commercially there. Long slow cooking is recommended. The fruit bodies grow up to 10 cm in diameter and persist for months, being found all the year round. They can be shaped like ears, saucers or cups. In dry weather they become very hard and shrunken; in wet weather they swell up and shed their spores. They should be gathered when in the more swollen state. The Jew's Ear is characteristically found on elder but can be found on other trees especially in North America. Elm and willow are favoured species. It grows on dead parts of the tree and does not attack the living wood.

Clavaria fistulosa, right, is found in winter. This is another fairy club of rather solitary habit. It is found in not more than twos or threes on branches and leaves especially those of beech. When it is young it is yellow and as it ages it reddens and finally becomes darkish brown.

The Horn of Plenty *Craterellus cornu-copioides, bottom right,* is another excellently flavoured fungus that is particularly easily dried. It is found among dead leaves in woods especially beech woodland. Like the Chantarelle it is easy to collect because it usually fruits very abundantly. At first sight it looks like old dirty black leather. This funereal appearance has given rise to the French name of Trompette des Morts.

The theme of edible species to be found in woodland continues here with more species characteristically found on beech.

Pleurotus ostreatus, top left, is known variously as the Oyster Cap, Oyster Fungus, Oyster Mushroom and Oyster Pleurotus. It does considerable damage as it is parasitic on hardwood trees, particularly beech. Found all the year round it is inclined to be tough and requires long cooking but dries well. It is possible to confuse it with its near relative *Pleurotus dryinus* (not illustrated). Such confusion is not dangerous but *Pleurotus dryinus* is not at all palatable. Its cap is white and scaly. The cap of the Oyster Fungus is blue, fading to pale fawn with age, and smooth.

Russula aurata or Golden Russula *centre.* *Russula* species are difficult to identify with confidence because of immense variation in colour from one individual to another. *Russula aurata* has a bright orange or red cap. *Russula vesca,* shown on page 16, is one of the easiest to recognise. Neither of these species are dangerous when cooked, when they taste excellent.

Boletus edulis, bottom left, the Cep or Penny Bun, Edible or King Boletus, is one of the most famous of all the edible fungi. The cap is variable in colour and can range from a pale creamy brown to quite a dark brown. The *Boletus* family is peculiar in that the members do not have mushroom-like gills but the spores are borne instead in a spongy mass of fine tubes leading from the cap. These pores are best scooped away before cooking. Ceps are much liked by insects and should be cut in half when preparing them for the table to make sure that fly maggots have not got there first. Picking them young gives the humans a better chance of getting there first themselves. Ceps are good fried or grilled and dry very well. It is possible that the Cep contains something that has the effect of retarding certain kinds of cancer but this has not been fully investigated. One of the problems is that the Cep cannot be successfully cultivated.

Cortinarius alboviolaceus, right, looks an extremely sinister fungus with its white and lilac colouring, but it can be quite safely eaten. It is found in autumn in oak as well as beech woods and is considered by some to have a better flavour than the Field Mushroom.

The first two species here are found in coniferous woods, the third at the edge of leafy woods. The edible theme continues.

Sparassis crispa, the Cauliflower Fungus *left,* is another club fungus. Its unmistakable cauliflower-like or spongy growth is found at the base of stumps in autumn. It has flat, twisted, and very divided branches. Young specimens are delicious when baked, and should be gathered when a pale cream colour. If yellow they are tough and indigestible.

Lactarius deliciosus, the Delicious Lactarius, Saffron Milk Cap or Orange-Milk Lactarius *below,* has, as might be expected, saffron-coloured milk. It is not generally considered as delicious as its name suggests but it is gathered for drying, particularly in Russia.

The Parasol Mushroom *Lepiota procera, right,* is intolerant of shade. It is unusual to find large numbers together. The cap has shaggy scales which are quite unlike the patches on *Amanita* caps and which do not rub off. It has a bulbous base and a large thick moveable double ring. The stringy stem is best discarded.

The edible theme draws to a close with three species all of which are found in a variety of habitats including grassland, hedgerows, banks, fields and woodland.

Calvatia saccata, left, a large common puff-ball found in autumn.

The Giant Puff-ball *Calvatia gigantea, below,* grows to become the largest fungus of all. The average North American specimen weighs about 14kg. As it grows older the Giant Puff-ball becomes yellow and then green. It should be eaten when young and white, sliced, and fried like steak. The French name, Tête de Mort, arose because some found in a field looked like bleached human skulls.

The Common Morel *Morchella esculenta, right,* is thought to favour ground which has been burnt. It is found in spring. The cap resembles a cross-section of a honeycomb or sponge. It often grows up through bare soil and can be dirty, so it should be well washed before thorough cooking. It is rather like *Gyromitra esculenta* (page 7) but the cap of this bulges, whereas the cap of the Morel is pitted.

Lactarius pyrogalus, left, the Fiery Milk Cap, is not edible but the photograph shows the milky secretion typical of all members of this genus. This particular species is characteristically found under hazel in autumn.

The cap of this toadstool *below,* has been cut in half and shows tunnels made by the fly maggots with which it is infested. This serves as a warning that insects should be watched out for, especially in those toadstools known to be particularly liable to attack, namely *Boletus* and *Russula* species. The specimen in the picture has pores and not gills and therefore belongs to the *Boletus* family.

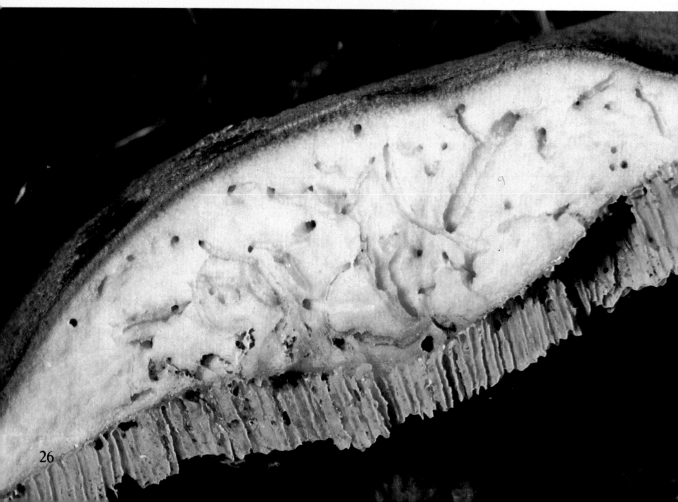

Fungi Parasitic on other Fungi

It may seem odd that fungi should be parasitic on other fungi. Yet the first species grows on an old and rotting host and the second does not seem to harm its host. Perhaps it would be more accurate to call the first a saprophyte – and who knows, the second relationship could prove to be symbiotic!

Nyctalis parasitica, the Pick-a-Back Toadstool, *right,* is a small fungus usually found in clusters on rotting species of *Russula* and *Lactarius.* It has thick, shallow, poorly-developed gills and gives off a most unpleasant smell.

Boletus parasiticus, below, is pictured on the Common Earth Ball *Scleroderma aurantium,* which is shown in more detail on page 53. *Boletus parasiticus* is normally found on earth balls, which do not appear to suffer from its presence. The cap is a rich olive-yellow with a velvety surface. The flesh and stem are yellow, the latter sometimes streaked with red. The stem is often bent at the point where it emerges from the earth ball.

Cup Fungi

The fruit bodies of cup fungi are quite different from anything already pictured. When they first appear they are closed, but then expand until they are cup or disc shaped. The spore-bearing surface or hymenium lines the cup, which either has a short stalk or rests directly on the ground. The spores are discharged upwards, triggered by wind or a touch. The flesh is gelatinous or elastic, and while many cup fungi are edible their appearance does not make them look particularly palatable.

Peziza aurantia, the Orange Peel Fungus, Orange Cup Fungus, Orange Elf Cup or Orange Fairy Cup *left,* is one of the largest and most striking of the cup fungi. It can reach up to 12 cm in diameter. It grows on damp bare soil or gravel in winter.

Sarcosypha coccinea, the Scarlet Elf Cup or Red Cup Fungus, *below,* is found on decaying twigs and branches in winter. It has short stems bearing goblet-shaped cups. These have a downy exterior, making the outside a pinky-white while the interior of the cups is red.

Right, Otidea auricula. The fruit bodies of members of the genus *Otidea* are shaped more or less like the ear of a hare or rabbit. They are found growing on the ground in woodland.

Fairy Clubs

Fairy Clubs are also known as Coral Fungi. None on these pages are as club-like as *Clavaria pistillaris* shown on page 17; the growth of some looks more like that of coral. The spore-bearing tissue covers the outer surface.

Clavaria vermicularis, left, is worm-like as its name suggests. It is very brittle and fragile and has no distinct stem. It is edible and found in grassy meadows in autumn.

Clavaria cristata, below, can be found in large numbers in frondose woods. The colour varies from white to pinkish or greyish.

Ramaria invallii, far right, is a leathery brown fairy club found in conifer plantations.

Clavaria amethystina, near right, is a brittle autumn species found in woods and on heaths among moss and grass.

Clavaria helvola, bottom right, has unbranched slender stems tapering downwards which are bright to orange yellow in colour.

Bracket Fungi

There are many different kinds of bracket fungi. The name is given to the shape of the growth which is very different from the basic toadstool or mushroom shape. Different bracket fungi are not necessarily closely related whereas the fairy clubs are; so are the cup fungi.

Bracket fungi are typically without stalks and grow on trees in shelf-like forms. The Oyster Fungus (page 20) is a gilled bracket fungus.

The Dryad's Saddle or Scaly Polypore *Polyporus squamosus, top left,* is a polypore rather than a gilled fungus. The hymenium producing the spores lines tubes opening into the air by pores in much the same way as in the genus *Boletus*. The derivation of the first common name is apparent from the picture. This is obviously the perfect shape and size for a dryad to ride in! Several of these brackets are usually found growing closely together or overlapping. Each can measure up to 30 cm across. They are usually found on elm from spring onwards but can also be seen on sycamore, maple, apple and ash. The fungus causes a white rot which makes studying and collecting dangerous procedures. The brackets are considered edible when young.

Polyporus hispidus, another polypore, *centre,* has shaggy hairs on its upper surface. It darkens in colour as it ages, going from yellowish brown to blackish. It is found from spring to late winter on trunks of leafy trees, particularly apple and ash. The snail feeding on the fungus is an example of the many different animals which feed on fungi. These range from mammals (e.g. squirrels and rabbits) to the many invertebrates which eat them, including woodlice, beetles, slugs and various flies.

Schizophyllum commune, the Common Schizophyllum or Common Split Gill, *bottom left,* is a gilled bracket fungus. This beautiful and delicate fan shape looks as though it has been made with mathematical precision. It can be found all the year round on hardwoods–on trunks, dead branches, newly-felled wood and stacked timber. It can revive on re-wetting after being dried out for long periods. Indeed specimens are reported to have been kept dry for 35 years in a vacuum after which they revived and produced viable spores.

This is one of several species of fungus which have proved important in genetic research.

The Sulphur Polypore *Polyporus sulphureus, right,* is one of the largest and most conspicuous of the bracket fungi sometimes attaining a diameter of 40 cm. The colour varies with age, the bright sulphur-yellow upper surface fading to a dirty white. It causes serious decay of the heartwood of a number of trees, especially oak. It is also commonly found on cherry and is one of the few fungi that grow on yew. Brackets first appear in the summer and many grow together overlapping each other. The flesh is thick and spongy with a strong smell and unpleasant taste.

Below, the Giant Polypore, *Polyporus giganteus.* The fruit body is composed of a number of fan-shaped branches each with its own stem but joining at a common base. It is found in groups measuring up to one metre across around the bases of various hardwood trees, especially oak and beech. The whitish pores blacken on ageing or if cut. It can be found in summer, autumn and winter.

34

Colourful Fungi

This section illustrates some of the many different and beautiful colours that fungi exhibit.

The delicate pinky-red gelatinous cups, *left*, of a cup fungus *Peziza* sp. were photographed in a tropical rainforest in Mexico.

The Verdigris Agarics *Stropharia aeruginosa* pictured *right and below* show how the shape of a fungus can vary at different ages, stressing the fact that shape should not be the sole factor used when determining identity. This particular fungus also varies in colour as it ages. The green colour is not visible while the young fungus is enclosed in its outer covering, the veil. It is washed off by the rain so old specimens can become a dull yellowish green. This is an unmistakable autumn fungus which appears in a variety of habitats including woods and grassland.

Amanita echinocephala, left, illustrates again some of the distinctive features of this dangerous genus. The remains of the volva are visible on the bulbous base of the stipe and studded with astonishing regularity in spiny warts on the top (*echinocephala* means hedgehog-headed).

Pholiota flammans, right, is found on decaying trunks or stumps of conifers.

The Parrot Wax Cap *Hygrophorus psittacinus, below,* is found in short grass in autumn. The cap and stalk are covered with a greenish slime when young, but as the toadstool ages yellow-ish or pinkish patches develop. The green colour is *not* caused by the presence of chlorophyll. The cap is bell-shaped at first; on expansion it measures about two cm across.

Microglossum viride, left, is an Earth Tongue. The club shaped structure carries the fertile layer and is supported by a slender stem. It appears in late autumn on soil in leafy woods.

Russula mairei, below left, is another Russula typically found in beech woods, It is very similar to *Russula emetica* (page 9) and to avoid unpleasant mistakes it is probably safer not to gather it for the table although it is reputed to have a good flavour.

Amanita excelsa is very like *Amanita pantherina* (page 7) but it is larger and the patches on the cap are grey rather than white, *below right.* It is a harmless woodland species found from mid-summer to autumn.

Coprinus disseminatus, the Brittle or Crumble Cap, *right,* is normally found growing in large clusters on or near the stumps of trees. Although it is a relative of the Ink Caps it does not liquefy but shrivels as it ages. It is found from early summer to late autumn.

The Fairy Umbrella or Little Wheel Toadstool *Marasmius rotula, left*, is found in clusters in woodland on decaying sticks in summer and autumn. It is rather small; the caps measure about 1 cm. The gills are joined to a collar around the top of the stem like the spokes of a wheel.

Below, Russula xerampelina. The specific name is derived from the Greek and means the colour of withered vine leaves. The colour is in fact very variable ranging from wine-red to purple and brown. There is a strong fishy smell from older specimens, which has been likened to that of crab, lobster or cooked shrimps. It is found in woods in late summer and autumn.

Right, Laccaria amethystea, the Amethyst Agaric, Amethyst Laccaria or Amethyst Deceiver. The beautiful deep violet of this toadstool makes it rather conspicuous in damp weather. The colour becomes duller and paler when the fungus is dry. It is found in deciduous woods in late summer and autumn.

Mitrula paludosa, above left, is very common in spring on decaying and submerged leaves on the mossy margins of ponds and streams.

The Waxy Laccaria or Waxy Deceiver *Laccaria laccata, below left,* is a common and very variable species of woods and heaths, found in summer and autumn. It is a very close relative of *L. amethystea* shown on the previous page but the colour tends to be grey to reddish-brown rather than violet. Both species are edible but the caps are small and the stalks so tough and stringy that it is necessary to discard them.

Pholiota destruens, far right, is as destructive as the name indicates. It grows mainly on poplars and causes a heart rot. It is found in late autumn.

Marasmius foetidus is shown growing on a rotten branch, *near right.* As would be expected from its name it has a foetid smell. It is usually found on beech or hazel in autumn.

The Scarlet Wax Cap or Scarlet Hood *Hygrophorus coccineus, bottom right,* is found in grassy places, especially near woods, from June onwards. The bell-shaped cap and flesh are at first cherry red but the colour soon fades to yellow.

43.

Tricholoma lascivum, left, is a gregarious species of deciduous woods, especially oak. It has a sweetish smell and taste which leaves a faintly gassy after-flavour. It appears in autumn.

Cortinarius paleaceus. This pretty fungus, *above right,* has an almost oriental look about it. Oddly enough it has a pronounced smell of geranium. This is another woodland species.

Members of the genus *Cortinarius* can be recognised when young because they have a web-like veil called the cortina passing from the stem to the cap and covering the gills. This is just discernible in the young toadstool in the picture on page 47.

Chlorosplenium aeruginascens. The blue-green cups of this fungus, *below,* appear on decayed wood, and the mycelium itself turns the wood green. This coloured wood has been used for marquetry (Tunbridge Ware). The fungus can be seen in autumn, particularly on oak but also on ash.

Little is known about the function of colour in fungi, making it an interesting subject for speculation. Colour could have similar functions to those in the plant and animal kingdom where it has often become an aid to the survival of the species. The survival of the individual (and hence the species) can sometimes depend on its camouflage to conceal it from predators. Some individuals use bold, bright colours to protect them; bright red in insects often marks that insect as evil-tasting if not actually poisonous. This is exploited by other insects whose colouration falsely protects them because it proclaims them to be unpalatable when they are really only mimics of poisonous species. Brightly coloured (and scented) flowers attract bees and other insects to them, resulting in pollination and the subsequent development of their seeds. The function of the fungal fruiting body is to liberate mature spores. It may therefore be to the fungus's advantage to be coloured so that it is inconspicuous and remains hidden from those who would make a meal of it before the spores are ripe. Alternatively it may be necessary to attract with bright colours (and strong smells) the insects and other animals that will eat the fungus and so ensure spore dispersal.

Cortinarius obtusus, above left, is a beautiful and delicate little fungus found mainly in conifer woods. The cap measures from one to four cm. It appears in the autumn.

Mycena alcalina, an elf-cap, *below left,* is even smaller than *Cortinarius obtusus.* It has a distinct nitric acid smell. It is found on and around tree stumps in late summer and autumn. It has been shown that at least eight other members of this genus are responsible for luminosity rather like that described for the Honey Fungus (page 16). The difference is that, rather than causing living trees to glow, these fungi make the decaying leaves and pine needles on the ground become luminous.

Cortinarius caerulescens, right, is a large species of *Cortinarius.* The cap reaches up to eight cm across. All parts are pale blue when young except the bulb at the base of the short thick stalk. The bluish-violet colour of the flesh soon fades and the cap becomes a watery brown. It is found in the deep litter of beech woods. Some people consider it to be edible.

The Wood Woolly-foot *Collybia peronata, left,* is so called because of the thick woolly hairs at the base of the stipe. It is a common saprophytic species of autumn woodland, particularly beech. The flesh has a strong peppery flavour.

Gyrodon lividus, below, is a rare species typically found in alder swamps. It is closely related to the *Boletus* genus. It rapidly becomes a vivid blue when damaged. It is possibly poisonous even when cooked.

Russula queletii, right, is a common but inedible species, possibly poisonous, usually associated with conifers. The cap is wine-red to violet and when old becomes spotted and greenish. It can be slimy. It has an acrid taste and a slightly sour smell may be apparent. The flesh discolours when broken. It is found in autumn.

Many Shapes and Sizes

Bird's Nest Fungi

It is not known what, if any, the advantage to the fungus could be of mimicking a bird's nest and eggs on such a minute scale. The mechanism of spore dispersal is however understood for these fungi. Each "egg" in the nest contains spores. During fairly heavy rain a raindrop falling into the cup has sufficient force to splash an "egg" from the cup and send it flying out. A thread spins out of the egg as the flight begins which entwines with anything it meets on its way e.g. grass, twigs, or the coat of an animal. The egg remains dangling until the spores are ready to disperse.

Cyathus striatus, the Striate Bird's Nest, *left*, has longitudinal furrows in the inside of the cup. It is found from spring to late autumn on dead wood, stumps, twigs and fir cones.

Cyathus olla, below, is more solitary in habit and has a smooth cup. It is found on soil, twigs etc. also from spring to late autumn.

Earth Stars

Earth Stars are closely related to Puff-balls and when young look very like them.

Right, Geastrum rufescens, the Common or Rosy Earth Star. Like more conventional-looking toadstools this too is the fruiting body growing from a mycelium. The outer layer splits and folds backwards as it dries and the spores are released through a hole in the top of the inner layer. While rare this species tends to occur in colonies, and so can be locally frequent, as can the species below.

Geastrum fornicatum. The extraordinary shape of this fungus, *below*, is only caused by the outer layer (exoperidium) folding back on itself. The spores are contained in a small puff-ball borne on a stalk supported by the four (or rarely five) legs of the exoperidium. It grows in grass, usually on the borders of woods. Both these species show a distinct preference for sandy soils.

The Peppery Milk Cap *Lactarius piperatus.* The odd shape here is just the freakish development of one particular toadstool, *left.* This white-capped toadstool is normally the usual funnel shape of all *Lactarius* species. As the name suggests the flesh is very peppery; indeed in some places the cap is crushed for use as a pepper substitute. It is found in broad-leaved woods in autumn.

Right, Lycoperdon echinatum, the Hedgehog or Spiny Puff-ball. The spines disappear when the fungus is old and weathered, leaving a well-marked pattern. This is not a very common puff-ball and is found in late summer and autumn in woods, especially beech.

The Common Earth-ball *Scleroderma aurantium, below,* is the species parasitised by *Boletus parasiticus* shown on page 27. It has been cut open to show the developing spores. In quantity it is poisonous and care should be taken not to confuse it with puff-balls. The bun-shaped fruit body can be 5-8 cm across, and old ones persist through the winter. They can be found from summer onwards in woods and heaths, not under dense tree cover.

The Dog Stinkhorn *Mutinus caninus, left,* is a near relative of the familiar Stinkhorn *Phallus impudicus* (not illustrated). These two, together with *Clathrus cancellatus* (sometimes known as the Cage Fungus or Lattice Stinkhorn), *top right,* rely on carrion-eating flies to disperse their spores. The cap of the Dog Stinkhorn is covered with a greenish mucus containing the spores but the smell of this is relatively slight. Although *Clathrus cancellatus* is one of the most attractive fungi in appearance, the olive-brown mucus inside the red hollow spherical lattice-work has a truly overpowering smell of bad meat. This stench attracts flies which feed on the mucus and thus distribute the spores.

The Dog Stinkhorn is common and found from July to November in woods, especially around stumps, and on rotting sawdust. It can sometimes be found on strawy manure heaps.

Clathrus cancellatus develops from an egg-shaped structure, the wall of which has three layers. The layers can be seen in the picture, the inner and outer ones thin, the middle one thick and gelatinous. In parts of France this fungus is thought to cause cancer, skin eruptions and convulsions.

Another odd-shaped fungus, *Sclerotinia tuberosa, below right,* attacks the rhizomes of both wild and cultivated species of Anemone. It is rather rare and can be found in spring.

On the left are three non-toadstool shapes, on the right delicate parasol shapes.

Trichoglossum hirsutum, top left, is an earth tongue which is found in acid grass in autumn.

Leotia lubrica is another earth tongue, *left centre,* found in this case in rich wettish soils in deciduous woods in autumn. It has gelatinous flesh and a smell reminiscent of the Chantarelle. The heads become very slimy in wet weather.

Helvella crispa, a relative of the Morels, is sometimes known as the False Morel, Saddle Fungus or Common Helvel, *bottom left.* It has odd saddle-shaped cups and is unusual, too, in that it can be found in both spring and autumn, although it is more common in autumn. It grows in damp frondose woods on rich soil, usually along paths. It contains the same poison as *Gyromitra esculenta,* but is supposed to be safe when cooked or dried.

Auriscalpium vulgare. This fragile-looking little toadstool, *far right,* is a tooth fungus of the same family as *Hydnum rufescens* (page 18), but it is very much smaller than the latter. It grows on pine cones and is found nearly all the year round.

The Magpie *Coprinus picaceus* is an ink cap, *right.* The white felty patches are formed as the expanding cap breaks the outer covering (the veil). The cap remains conical for spore discharge and deliquesces. The Magpie is typically found in beech woods in autumn but is rather rare.

Mycena galericulata, the Capped Mycena or Grey Bonnet Mycena, *below right,* is an elf-cap. As well as the luminosity discussed on page 46 this genus is also noted for its hallucinogenic qualities, although the delicate white caps could hardly look less ominous. *Mycena galericulata* can be found clustered on tree stumps, especially alder and birch. It is common and appears all the year round.

These three pictures illustrate variations on the basic toadstool shape. While all are scaly and much the same colour the final effect in each case is very different.

Lepiota clypeolaria, left, is characterised by concentric rings of granular scales which give it its pale brownish colour. The stem has a felty appearance. This small *Lepiota* is classified as edible but it is not really worth eating. It is found in autumn in woods on needle cover or deep foliage.

The Shaggy Pholiota *Pholiota squarrosa, right,* is an autumn species, found in dense tufts at the base of deciduous trees, particularly birch, which it kills. It too has scales which are dark and which grow on both cap and stem. It is edible but indigestible.

Below, Tricholoma aurantium. The cap is smooth but the stipe is very scaly. It is found in coniferous woods in autumn, often in fairy rings.

59

Clitocybe infundibuliformis, the Common Funnel Cap, *left*, has an attractive funnel-shaped cap when mature although it is convex when young. This species can vary in colour from pink to yellow to tan. It is usually found in woods in late summer and autumn. It can resemble the Chantarelle (page 16) but it is much less solid and the gills are white and not yellow. It is often found in fairy rings in summer and autumn.

Coprinus micaceus, the Glistening Ink Cap, is shown, *below and right*. This is another example of how the appearance of different individuals of the same species can vary. The young cap is scattered with glistening mica-like scales, but these disappear as the cap darkens and dries out. Unlike the Magpie (page 57) the cap does spread for spore discharge. Unlike other ink caps very little auto-digestion takes place. This fungus is common and is found on and around stumps of broad-leaved trees from spring to autumn.

Strobilomyces floccopus, known in North America as the Pine Cone Fungus, *top left,* is easily identified by the very large blackish overlapping scales on its cap. On exposure to the air the white flesh turns reddish and then blackish. It is like *Boletus* species in having vertical tubes opening below by pores rather than radiating gills. The cap is nearly spherical when young, and then flattens to resemble a pine cone.

The Wood Puff-ball, Stump Puff-ball or Pear-shaped Puff-ball *Lycoperdon pyriforme, bottom left,* is the only British species of puff-ball that grows on wood, being found on woody stumps or buried wood. The young are pear-shaped, often found in groups. They are covered with small whitish spines or granules which soon disappear, so the mature puff-balls are smooth, like the Giant Puff-ball (page 24). The spores are discharged through pores at the top, unlike the members of the genus *Calvatia,* which includes the Giant Puff-ball. Here the top of the ball breaks away into irregular pieces allowing the spores to be released. It has been calculated that a Giant Puff-ball releases as many as 7,000,000,000,000 (7×10^{12}) spores, but all fungi produce an astonishing number. It is likely that a mushroom 10 cm across will release 1,600,000,000 (16×10^{8}) spores in the few days of its existence.

Collybia dryophila, the Russet Shank or Penny Top, *right,* is a delicate little toadstool which must surely provide an ideal resting place for a fairy. It resembles the Fairy-ring Champignon (page 13) but has a different habitat, being found in summer and autumn in deciduous woods, especially oak.

INDEX

First published in Great Britain 1978 by Colour Library International Ltd.,
Designed by David Gibbon. Produced by Ted Smart. © Text: Jacqueline Seymour. © Illustrations: Frank W. Lane and Bruce Coleman Ltd.
Colour separations by La Cromolito, Milan, Italy. Display and Text filmsetting by Focus Photoset, London, England.
Printed and bound by L.E.G.O. Vicenza, Italy. All rights reserved. ISBN No. 0 904681 43 2
COLOUR LIBRARY INTERNATIONAL